I0441249

When Families Go Wrong

James Nugent

Disclaimer

Millions of people live with unhappy and chaotic families. In this book you may recognize your issues. Readers are strongly cautioned that no booklet can substitute for professional personal and spiritual counseling. If you have any of these issues get help. The penalty paid for not taking action may be a lifetime of misery.

This means that we must somehow put to rest the disappointments and emotional injuries of childhood. Strangely in many families the chaos and pain continue for the rest of their lives.

About the Author

James Nugent spent 31 years as a certificated teacher and or school counselor. He also spent 22 years as a counselor in part time private practice. In that time he saw the damage inflicted on children and suffered by adults; when they have unhappy families gone wrong.

About the Book

This is a book about all the families that fail to nurture their members. It is not about: criminal neglect, physical abuse, or sexual abuse. It is about emotional abuse but not the kind that usually gets reported to Children's Protective Services.

In fact, although the groundwork may be laid in childhood; this book is about what siblings inflict on each other in adulthood. It is about abusive and disrespectful behavior and about people who don't feel free to walk away.

When a child emancipates from a family there is a myth that the nurturing role of the family is concluded. It is not. In order to be a healthy and happy adults; we must all live abuse free and that means we need a nurturing family in which to fall back. From this home base we can go physically and emotionally far and wide.

It is like a boat that leaves the dock, and sails through storms and visits exotic places. Eventually the boat and the adult child will return home briefly in order to rest and make sense of the adventures and sea. For many people and families there is no safe harbor.

Although not a substitute for competent counseling, this book may be a starting point for discussion about families which go wrong.

Note

Although all people and examples used in this book are true to life; all identifying characteristics have been changed. It is impossible that I am talking about you personally. However the "type of character" presented in this booklet may through coincidence bear a striking resemblance to you or your family or your life. If this is so; I will have done my job as an educator and writer. Run with this new insight, to a professional for help and make your life excellent.

Authors Note

I have wanted to write about families that went wrong for a long time. But I was stopped by a fear of inflicting more pain on the victims. So, let me be perfectly clear. You deserve to be treated with care, courtesy and respect. If you aren't treated with, care, courtesy and respect even by family; you have the right to terminate the relationship or modify the relationship.

Unhappy Holidays

The holidays were six months away and many families will be spending time together. The holidays are typically difficult times for many families and individuals. For the most part, while an endless stream of images of "perfect" families play on our TV screens; most of us feel dissatisfied because we don't achieve anything near the ideal family. These unrealistic expectations cause wide spread suffering. The pain is a frequent topic in counseling offices especially during the holidays.

When Families Go Wrong

There is another cause of; shame, acute emotional pain and anger. These families are holding millions of full grown adult as emotional hostages. These families hold out the promise of love and belonging and provide a hellish experience of emotional abuse. Rarely does anybody get physically abused.

The victims stay hooked because they blame themselves and they try to fix the relationships. Of course the abusers have no motivation to change. The abusers like the power they have and aren't going to let it go. If their target for bullying stepped out of their assigned role; the bully might be the new target of abuse when families go wrong. No, everybody except the victim wants everything to stay the same. The crazier the emotional abuse, the stronger the motivation for victims to return to their families, and try to fix it.

Jamie's Clan

Jamie was a 30 year old professional woman. She had four sisters. Jamie was particularly close to her youngest sister. They spent at least five nights a week together. They would go to the movies, drink, smoke pot, party and even visit the casino when they had money.

Both women have had difficult marriages and are divorced. They each have two children (all girls). Parenting was not their priority.

Jamie's little sister's name is Lea. Lea lies. She manipulates and torments everybody in her life with lies. She even started a rumor that her mother sexually molested Jamie. She also told Jamie that her mother confided in her and that she didn't feel comfortable with Jamie around. Jamie stays away from her mother because of this lie. Over the years the rumor about sexual molestation has been twisted into a greatly expanded tales involving a cast of a dozen.

Jamie is treated like dirt by her other siblings. They mocked her in front of her. Nothing she does is good enough. She repeatedly went to family events and was tormented. She couldn't seem to walk away. Jamie was in such distress that she came to my office for general unhappiness.

About this time Jamie found a potential husband. Lea worked hard to drive a wedge between the two. Frank was a hard working psychiatrist, who wanted a peaceful home life and a loving marriage. Frank knew that marrying Jamie and making a solid life together, was a long shot. Yet Jamie had many characteristics that made her an ideal partner for Frank.

For example, she liked to share with the less fortunate. She had the habit of instantly and lovingly sharing with others. Frank was a generous person too and had seemingly infinite patience.

In his work and his life he was thrilled to watch people grow, and be happy. After a few years and numerous conflicts with Jamie's family they decided to wed. There was one issue that had to be dealt with.

Lea had to be banned from their home and time spent with Lea had to be reduced to 2 nights a week. Frank was firm in his request. The wedding would be called off if he didn't get what he wanted. He was not going to allow Lea to lie and abuse people in his own home. It was a risky stand but Frank felt he had no choice. The Chaos and abuse had to stop. He was not joining an abusive family.

Jamie decided to start a new life. She literally ran away from her family. She decided to marry Frank. Her self-esteem went up. Almost immediately because she expected courtesy and respect from everyone in her life; she got raises at work. These raises and promotions continue to this very day some 10 years later. There seems to be a correlation between her self-esteem and how she is treated at work.

Over time Jamie stopped hanging out with Lea. One day she told Frank, "Why would I want to do that?"

Over the years Jamie got better friends. Her social life became much more rewarding. Her daughters grew up in a healthy abuse free environment, and even as adults have not associated with the monsters in Jamie's family of origin.

Occasionally Frank and Jamie attend family funerals and weddings but now they feel more like tourists at the zoo. They definitely do not feel like victims, anymore.

Reflections

I was involved with this family on and off for a number of years. I really thought Frank made a mistake and he was trying to fix what went wrong in his own similar family of origin. Upon reflection I think I was wrong. He just was trying to form a loving family with Jamie and her two daughters. It worked so far.

Jimmy's Family

Jimmy was a 28 year old single. He was prone to anxiety attacks and never was able to maintain a happy relationship. When he came to my office he reported that he was depressed and isolated and unhappy.

I asked him about his family of origin and he reported that his mother and father were emotionally distant and his brothers were over the top competitive. They apparently competed for the attention and love of their parents. It was attention and love that never came. Jimmy was rejected and bullied by his brothers until he left the home at 18 years old.

As an adult, the abuse from his brothers never stopped. Jimmy's car was never good enough. They had wives; he didn't. They laughed at him. They were cruel in their insults.

Modestly successful in his work as a preschool teacher; he had acute low self-esteem and his fear of authority figures hindered his interaction with administrators.

He asked me to help clean up the effects of his childhood. I told him that we could definitely work on his anxiety and his sadness. He would need to re-parent himself, and that might take quite some time. I taught him reality therapy strategies for dealing with distressing emotions.

He took to the concepts and quickly developed the skills to manage the symptoms. Reality Therapy is basically a cognitive therapy approach. If we change how we think about something we can change our emotions and our behavior. It is a very liberating approach. Jimmy made amazing progress in just a month.

The holidays came around and Jimmy was sent into a tail spin. Just the thought of spending Thanksgiving and Christmas with his brothers started to make him wish he could die. I explained that we could replace his thoughts and feelings with something happy. I also off handedly mentioned that it was not required that he visit and be emotionally abused by his brothers or his distant parents. He smiled and then laughed.

He said that maybe it is time that he look for and participate in a loving family. Perhaps he knew what he really wanted in life.

We started with Thanksgiving. He didn't go. However on my advice he did not stay home and sulk. He decided to go to a local community kitchen and help serve the homeless. The next week he reported that he had a great time and felt a kinship with the homeless people. They were all without family too! He was rather peaceful about the whole thing. I encourage him to keep that upbeat feeling as we entered December.

The next week he had a plan for Christmas and New Year's Eve. He had signed up for a two week mission trip in Tijuana Mexico. He would be a guest of the Catholic Church and spend the holidays with people like himself, doing good for others. We put a backup plan in place just in case the first plan didn't work out. Off my client went to a strange and different land. I actually worried a tiny bit about him while he was gone. But sometimes the client really knows what is best!

Upon Jimmy's return he had one last appointment. He thanked me and assured me he would come again to counseling if he was controlled by anxiety or depression again. He said that he was now the designer of his life and was choosing a life free of abuse and emotional distress. I reminded him to make sure he used his new tools. It would be a while before they were a helpful habit.

Epilog

Jimmy sent a postcard to me years later. He never did see his brothers or parents again. He now resides in San Blas Mexico. He is a dive instructor and has a wife two children. He became a Roman Catholic and was married in Mexico. He said that Catholics marry for life and he invited none of his family of origin to the wedding.

Reflections

In the two stories above the people decided to terminate their relationships with their families. Sometimes this is the only way a person can carve out a happy life. It is important that when one leaves an abusive relationship that they get professional support. Otherwise they are likely to find themselves in another abusive relationship. Abused people are very likely to repeat the same scenes over and over because it is what they are used to. Abuse is crazy making. Get healed of your deep wounds before striking up new relationships.

Some people are able to eliminate abusive/problem people from their lives and still maintain reasonable relationships with other survivors. Once again I did not necessarily agree with the following client's plan for improving her life; but counseling is always client directed.

Sara's Clan

Sara came from a large family. She had nine siblings. The children basically raised themselves. Mental illness and substance abuse was rampant in the family. Mom and dad are a bit of a mystery but they were reputed to be very needy and not in charge.

Some of the children left home as soon as they were able. Other siblings stayed as long as they could until they were literally put out on the sidewalk. Two of the siblings got to stay several years longer because they were allegedly struck down with schizophrenia. One of the two died of an accidental overdose of meth. The other, Billy began to control all the other people in the family.

His mantra was always the same. Give me what I want, because I'm mentally ill. This tactic worked even with the police. Billy could tear up restaurants or steal thing from stores and then scream, "You can't touch me. I am mentally ill." It being a small town, this behavior was more or less tolerated. Although Billy was officially banned from some establishments; basically he got his way.

Inside the family, if anyone dared to disappoint Billy; they had hell to pay from the other siblings. If Billy demanded a ride or money; it was easiest to give it to him. It seems quite ridiculous but those are the facts according to Sara. Billy still lived at home with his parents.

I asked Sara if she wanted to escape from this abusive relationship with her siblings. She didn't answer. Shortly thereafter, her parents died in a car accident.

Sara wanted to use the estate to provide for Billy, but there wasn't a will and the siblings were not in a mood to share the estate anyway. The six siblings converged on the beautiful lake house and looted it while Billy was out annoying the neighborhood. The house was on a second mortgage and went back to the bank.

Sara wanted to save one relationship in this abusive family. His name was Dan. Of all her siblings he was the one that never abused her directly. I pointed out that perhaps by default he allowed her to be abused. She forgave him and still wanted to have a relationship. I advised extreme caution.

She chatted with him and it was decided the she was welcome in his home and he was allowed in her home. They would strike up a friendship and see if there was any possibility of them having a familial relationship in the future.

As for her other siblings, Sara would reluctantly have little or no contact. If somebody chose to get therapy and was willing to give up abusive behavior; Sara was willing to include them in her new family.

In counseling, Sara developed a list of expectations (rules) for how she was to be treated by other people. I eventually had them put on a poster which I placed on my office wall. Sara's self-esteem soared as she felt empowered to enforce her rules.

Epilog

To date, several years later, she has a non-abusive (loving) husband and they are trying to have babies. Dan is a fixture around their house and engaged to be married to a wonderful abuse survivor.

Reflection

In my years as a counselor there were few individuals that escaped abusive relationships permanently. They almost always jumped from one abusive relationship directly the next. I also watched a general trend of people moving from being an emotional abuse victim, to a physical or sexual abuse victim. The final outcome if uninterrupted seems to be: self-inflicted death, homicide by abuse, or catastrophic medical problems induced by stress.

People do escape abuse, but many are worn down to the point where they are simply killed by it.

It makes the most sense to escape it as soon as one recognizes it. Get help and get out immediately. Otherwise it ends very poorly.

Final Thoughts About When Families Go Wrong

Families are supposed to support the emotional health of their members.

Families should never ridicule members.

Families should not inflict emotional pain on members.

If a family member persists in abusive behavior; they can and should be expelled.

If a family allows emotional abuse; members have the right to leave.

You have a right to be treated with courtesy, respect, and care.

If your family is emotionally abusive; it is their fault, not yours.

There are many competent counselors who will assist you in making your escape. Start the conversation. You can reject abuse and be free of it.

Best regards

James Nugent

7-12-15

Notes

Books by James Nugent

When Families Go Wrong

Kayak at Dawn

Are Catholics Going to Hell?

Catholic Marriage and Conflict Resolution

Home Self-defense

How to Get Work

Fermenting Milk and Sprouting Beans in J.J.'s Kitchen

The Beach Cabin

Paddling to the Rhythm of God

Campfires at the Beach

Rainy Day Kayak

The Catholic Way of Dying

Advanced Social Jujitsu

Deep Catholic Morality

Paddles and Water

The Power of Habits

The Beginning School Counselor

Learning My Limits in Small Craft Boating

Eight Things You Need to Survive

Writing My First Books

How I Sailed From Olympia to the San Juan Islands, and Returned Safely

An Alternative Boating Guide to Southern Puget Sound

How and Why I Lived Aboard

Kayaking Budd Inlet in South Puget Sound

Night Kayaking

Writing E-books and Making the Perfect Book

I Speak Esperanto

The Rainbow Road and Other Signs of God's Love

Living an Abundant Life, Within Your Means

Social Jujitsu and Powerful Principles for Managing Social Conflict

Blackjack on My Small Budget

A Little Benedictine Oblate Manuel

Without Speech

All things work

Loving Time with Your Creator

Personal Adventures in a Life of Learning

The Good News about Being Catholic

E-book Writing and Overcoming Barriers to Creativity

E-book Writing and Organizing Your Ideas

My Forty Days for Life 2013

Lifestyle Reality Observing

How to Sail in the Winter

How to Get Your Kid to Move Out

I built a Raft

How to Get What Want

Sex, Abstinence, and Happiness

Cynthia Says Radio Show – Anger is a choice

More Good News about Being Catholic

The Solo Kayak

A Beach Naturalist on Southern Puget Sound

Clean House Clean Life

The Total Catholic Christian

Happiness is a Choice

Life in Young Cove

Solo Kayak II

The Extraordinary Eucharistic Visitor

Available at Amazon.com in Kindle E-Book and or Audible Book or Paperback

All rights reserved. Copyright 2015 Eld Inlet Services

www.ingramcontent.com/pod-product-compliance
Lightning Source LLC
Chambersburg PA
CBHW070300300526
45791CB00022B/1673